I0792612

REVIEWS

"The author has crafted a well-developed guide that will broaden the landscape for traditional healers and clinicians interested in holistic therapeutic modalities! I resonated with his FAITH acronym, where you honor healing as a sacred inside job. Well done, Dr. Figueroa."

Dr. Amelia Kemp, PhD, licensed psychotherapist

"Dr. Figueroa's book maintains his unique style of harmonizing contrasting views when dwelling in the complex field of therapeutic styles while creating a self-healing manual for all practitioners. He shares his experience in facilitating healing without controlling the process of how it should occur. This manual will guide all practitioners to find their inner healers."

Carli Muñoz, musician, composer, and author

"What a beautiful read! This is a very insightful and empowering book for all therapists. Thank you, Dr. Figueroa."

Elspeth Kerr, holistic therapist in Paphos, Cyprus

"As a Buddhist reading the material of Dr. Figueroa, it is a stimulating exercise to review one's philosophy and practice. The material is well thought out. For those interested in a nonreligion-based investigation into the nature of our being, it is a good work. Common sense pervades the whole presentation."

Jhampa Shaneman, Buddhist lama and astrologer

"*Spirituality 201: Discovering the Inner Healer* by Ivan Figueroa-Otero is a step-by-step guide to holographic healing and an advanced curriculum for holistic health seekers working toward helping others restore their health. In this second level of the School of Life curriculum, Figueroa-Otero delves deep into the root causes of diseases, explaining why the equilibrium of our health becomes unbalanced, and offers in-depth insights to therapists on how to approach the recovery process. This is one of the most unique self-help books I've ever read. Figueroa-Otero focuses on the symbiotic relationship of the human body and its consciousness with the larger universe and how it affects us spiritually, mentally, and physically. A must-read for therapists and patients alike."

Reviewed by Pikasho Deka for Readers' Favorite

"I liked *Spirituality 201* because it focuses on understanding the theory and the practice. At the end of each chapter, Figueroa-Otero includes review questions that allow readers to meditate on what they have learned. He explains why emotional wounds need spiritual and mental focus to heal. A topic that I found interesting is self-esteem. He explains how wisdom grows with our mistakes and our successes in the same manner. That is why we should not have regrets when we make a mistake but seek to master it with knowledge gained from experience. The author reminds us that both meditation and prayer clear our minds because they allow communication with God. This book is helpful because it guides the inner development of the self through understanding."

Reviewed by Diana Lopez for Readers' Favorite

"In this manual for therapists, Dr. Figueroa has shared what has facilitated the healing process in his patients to support other colleagues in their varied therapeutic roles. He emphasizes facilitating the healing process by using empathy as a compassionate placebo. Although my practice relies on science-based alternatives, I believe my patients will benefit from his recommendations."

Alejandro Perez, MD, ABMS, FAAPMR, MPH, ABAARM

OTHER BOOKS BY IVÁN FIGUEROA-OTERO

Spirituality 101:

For the Dropouts of the School of Life:

A Review for the Final Exam

Spirituality 1.2:

For the Disconnected from the School of Life:

A Review for Tekkies

Spirituality 103:

The Forgiveness Code:

Finding the Light in Our Shadows

Spirituality 104:

Reflections in My Magical Mirror: Lessons of Love from the School of Life

To all the teachers, disciples, and patients whom I have participated with in the School of Life, inspiring me to share all their experiences, especially my patients and their testimonies of love and lessons learned. That led me to find the key to forgiveness and penetrate the healing code of the soul's genome to share the vast wisdom that springs lovingly from it. My progress in the universal classroom would not have been possible without them. That motivated me to share it with others in gratitude.

If you rediscover the distorted light created by your fears in the reflection of this book's pages, share the merit and learning with your fellow students in the School of Life.

www.mascotbooks.com

Spirituality 201: Discovering the Inner Healer: A Self-Healing Manual for Therapists

©2023 Iván Figueroa-Otero. All Rights Reserved. No part of this publication may be reproduced, stored in a retrieval system or transmitted in any form by any means electronic, mechanical, or photocopying, recording or otherwise without the per-mission of the author.

This book is not intended as a substitute for the medical advice of physicians. The reader should regularly consult a physician in matters relating to their health and particularly with respect to any symptoms that may require diagnosis or medical attention.

For more information, please contact:
Mascot Books, an imprint of Amplify Publishing Group
620 Herndon Parkway, Suite 220
Herndon, VA 20170
info@mascotbooks.com

Library of Congress Control Number: 2023906583

CPSIA Code: PRV0423A

ISBN-13: 978-1-63755-832-4

Printed in the United States

SPIRITUALITY 201

DISCOVERING THE INNER HEALER

A SELF-HEALING MANUAL FOR THERAPISTS

IVÁN FIGUEROA-OTERO, MD

CONTENTS

POEM

Health: The Unbalancing Equilibrium of Love

Ivan Figueroa Otero, MD

For the Inclusive Consciousness of Love,
there is no inappropriate action.
There are only unbalancing balances alternating with unceasing balancing imbalances,
where the continuous change results from
the entropy of love.
It is like the hugs we share when we
welcome or send a loved one on their
journey, which permanently supports
both, no matter the emotional result of
the encounter.
That is why symptoms or diseases only
balance imbalances resulting from our

intentions. Inclusive aims based on the benefit of the we experience generate all-pleasing changes for all, and unpleasant ones are created by the exclusive actions based on the attachment to the *mine*.

All occurrences, like embraces in departures and arrivals, benefit both *ours* and *mine*, even if they do not seem so from their perspectives.

That is why health and disease symptoms are only balances and imbalances for holographic welfare, just as climate disasters are for the planet.

And the feelings of well-being and discomfort associated with equilibrating corrections are just alarms that alert us to maintain the harmony of the hologram.

For, in the universal creative holographic process, every manifestation is nothing more than the entropy of love. That seeks to restore to holographic consciousness the dream state of the universal hologram that initially was free from the experience of duality. Falsely created by attachment to the memory of what we were before the great awakening of the creative explosion of Love.

GLOSSARY

1. **Matter:** Anything that takes up space and can be weighed and measured. It is the world we can see without physical senses.

2. **Antimatter:** The opposite of matter, which science postulates existed in equal amounts with the matter after the big bang but which scientists have lost track of since then. It is believed to give rise to matter, but they do not know how. At present, antimatter is undetectable by scientific measurements.

3. **Chaos:** A scientific theory that explains that the outcome of something depends on different variables and that it is impossible to predict. For example, if we place an egg on the cusp of a pyramid, we will not know where it will fall. Like quantum theory, the subjectivity of the observer's perception makes absolute predictive concordance of any observed fact impossible.

4. **Entropy:** The yang energy—the universal separating centrifugal force that seems chaotic and disorganized to the observer. According to the laws of physics, it is the tendency to return to the disorder, the energy systems, as they were found in their original state.

5. **Synergy:** The yin energy—the universal centripetal unifying force makes it easy for us to assemble our puzzle out of the apparent chaos of yang energy.

6. **Big bang:** This is the most accepted explanation by the scientific community to explain the origin of our universe. It postulates that the universe originated from the point of mass densification or singularity, where nothing existed but from where everything would arise. This book represents the incredible explosion of love stemming from the Great Dream of the transcendental mind upon awakening—to share all the accumulated wisdom of the previous creative cycle of the universe.

7. **Singularity:** A singularity means when *a point in time becomes infinite or immeasurable*. For

example, at the center of a black hole, according to classical theory, the density is infinite, because a finite mass is compressed to a zero volume. Hence it is a singularity.

8. **Interdependence (butterfly effect):** A concept describing the interaction between the parts of a holographic universe, where the action or reaction of one part of the universe affects the other components, like the effect of a wave (ripple effect) that as a chain reaction spreads throughout the universal holographic space. Like that described by quantum entanglement and the phrase of the Three Musketeers, "One for all and all for one." This is due to the subjectivity of the affected experience in dreams, as the butterfly effect describes within the apparent disorder of universal entropy.

9. **Time:** Time is a subjective definition of the observer's experience when interpreting a series of events with one's five senses. It is based on the brain's memory capacity, which divides them into imaginary (virtual) segments of the present, past, and future. To determine the weather, we use references to observable changes in the seasons (climates)

and the day-and-night rotation. Based on these changes, humanity has divided time into seconds, minutes, hours, days, months, years, centuries, etc.

10. **Time continuum:** The space-time continuum consists of four dimensions: the three dimensions of space (length, width, and height, plus the fourth dimension of time. Einstein's theories of relativity spurred other scientists to investigate the relationships between space and time. In my more straightforward interpretation, to create an experience in time, the only requirement is the memory of each of the occurrences that have passed. This implies that individual consciousness is needed to perceive or create the experience of time.

11. **Genome:** The set of genes in chromosomes (DNA), which can be interpreted as the complete biological, genetic information stored by a particular organism or species. It originates from the Latin *genus*, meaning "lineage."

12. **Biological-material DNA:** The biological genomic material or historical archive that

holds the entire human experience. Traditionally, the nucleic genetic content has been divided into a functional encoding part, which occupies 3 to 5 percent, and a nonfunctional or nonencoded, called garbage for its cosmetic role, which paradoxically inhabits 95 to 97 percent of the total.

13. **Exclusive intention:** The action guided by selfishness, where all causes and their effects influence the parts that make up the universe. This action generates suffering (corrective learning experience), both in the subject and object, caused by the attachment to the past, present, and future virtual reality.

14. **Inclusive intention:** The action guided by love (inclusiveness), in which the self recognizes that all causes and effects (results) affect all parts equally. As Jesus's words implied in Mathew 25:40: "Truly I tell you, whatever you did for one of the least of these brothers and sisters of mine, you did for me." This action generates happiness in both the object and the subject.

15. **Ego:** In Latin, it means "the self." This book refers to the self, making us feel like individuals and observers of the universe (individualism). It allows us to perceive what is our own and others, and observe the effects of time (birth, age, sickness, and death) and classify the quality of life with the feelings generated by our five senses into good and bad experiences, which influence our personality.

16. **Selfishness:** How a person exists, based on apparent independence and individualism. Occasionally, people feel falsely separated into races, colors, religions, knowledge, and power, where our actions and their effects are not observed as interdependent.

17. **Attachment:** The emotional need or habit to repeat enjoyable experiences, physically or mentally. In its most immature form, this may be the worst addiction human beings can perceive, and it is the primary source of their suffering. It may be an appropriate sensation in some cases and inappropriate in others.

18. **Epigenetics:** A branch of biology explaining why living organisms express (activate) some genetic characteristics and silence others—to form their physical features and their susceptibility to developing certain diseases. This contrasts with the deterministic concept of any genetic predisposition, suggesting that external factors, such as lifestyles, could influence DNA to change its actions without altering its genetic configuration. It is suspected that these changes are controlled by the junk DNA I refer to as luminous.

19. **Spiritual epigenetics:** The practice of remembering the most inclusive intentions and actions learned during the universal experience to perfect our material genome to obtain holographic harmony on all its parts.

20. **Mutation:** Mutation is any variation in the original structure of the genetic code that alters the genes of the chromosomes. They are an adaptation of the genetic code by the good, bad, or toxic influences the living organism is exposed to, which alters the species' state of health and survival. Not all are actively manifested and can only be triggered by the specific

effects of a given lifestyle's influence on the individual.

21. **Free will:** An individual's ability to exercise self-determination. Free will is different for everyone: it varies according to their level of spiritual development, intelligence, social situation, politics, ethics, and individual health. It is associated with an individual's ability to act with relative freedom according to the options available during their interdimensional journey. This vision, when focused on individualism, is known as selfishness.

22. **Hologram:** Three-dimensional projection obtained from a flat image by laser beam techniques. Today it is used on television to transmit a person's image to distant places. Soon we will see this technology in our homes. The important thing is to understand that scientist Dr. David Bhom established that the entire original could be reproduced from any part of an object or the universe. This suggests that the information of the image is contained in each of its features. This implies a form of intrinsic communication that does not depend on time and space.

23. **Holographic universe:** It has the characteristics of a hologram, and all its parts are interdependent with the others in a relationship such as that described by quantum entanglement. The experience of each component results in an inevitable interrelated effect on all others. This could be described as the Three Musketeers effect: "One for all and all for one."

24. **Multiverse:** A hypothetical group of multiple universes. Together these universes comprise everything that exists: the entirety of space, time, matter, energy, information, and the physical laws and constants that describe them. The different universes within the multiverse are called parallel universes, other universes, alternate universes, or many worlds. Universes within their multiverse maintain the holographic laws that govern their interdependency.

25. **Bioethics:** The branch of ethics dedicated to promoting ethical behavior within science and medicine. It includes aspects of human life and the rest of living creatures and the environment in which acceptable conditions can occur. This can be considered a holographic

integration of health that integrates the spiritual with the biological.

26. **Butterfly effect:** This concept refers to the notion of sensitivity to initial conditions within the framework of the chaos theory. Its name comes from a Chinese proverb: "The swirling of a butterfly's wings can be felt on the other side of the world." In a hologram where the tendency to entropy (chaos) naturally exists, an insignificant event, like a butterfly flapping its wings, can be amplified in other distant parts of the hologram.

27. **Law of cause and effect (law of love):** The impersonal application of Newton's third law to the experiences resulting from the actions of individual holograms during their interdimensional journey.

28. **The law of conservation of energy:** The law of conservation of energy states that energy can neither be created nor destroyed—only converted from one form of energy to another.

29. **Quantum entanglement:** An observable phenomenon regarding the relationship between individual particles that interact in an interdependent quantum state, where the reactions of a group of individual particles exhibit a group response as if they were physically and energetically connected, and as if there were no physical separation between them. They seem to be interconnected, notwithstanding the difference between them. The responses of individual particles would seem instantaneous without a measurable temporal separation.

INTRODUCTION

I congratulate all those who have reached level 201, a more comprehensive phase of the second level of our School of Life, because they were not frightened by the intensity of the exams or by their fellow students progress in their levels of learning.

At level 101, we encouraged readers to answer the three questions that arise during our journey: Who are we? Where do we come from? And where are we headed? Through the analysis of our individual experiences, scientific evidence, and the philosophies outlined by the great sages who preceded us along the way, we attempted to search the deepest parts of ourselves, where the answers spontaneously arise. In the first book, we emphasized that every failure resulted in the process of learning, which allowed us to restructure our curriculum to continue taking the exams incessantly until we learned the lesson. These examinations should not be seen as punishment but as loving acts of patience and confidence in our ability to pass them. Remember: the dropouts were the ones who gave up and stopped taking their exams.

At level 1.2, we wanted to address younger minds, for whom daily perspective is more based on modern technology. That is why we transformed the traditional scientific and religious vision into a more cybernetic one. In this text, we became programmers and navigators of cyberspace, which varied in their individual experiences according to the programs' purity or degree of corruption. Therefore, the best way to improve our personal browsing experience is to renew it, update our "software," and debug our operating systems for any viral invasion. In each of the above books, we introduced techniques that would facilitate reprogramming and learning, which we will continue to deepen as we publish the following levels.

At level 103, we discovered new perspectives on the three questions in level 101. We discussed intensely and in detail the causes and techniques that would help us effectively eradicate any viral contamination or guilt from our minds, which we had been responsible for inadvertently allowing into our learning programs. These alterations could be compared to emotional smudges in the mirror of our soul, which have not yet healed, suffered during the journey.

At level 104, *Reflections in My Magical Mirror: Lessons of Love from the School of Life,* we conducted a detailed review of all the lessons of the first three levels. But it is also a complete compendium for those advanced students arriving from other schools who wish to join the next advanced level of the new trilogy without reading the first books. After reading the selection of fifty-two phrases and their discussion, the new disciples may decide whether to continue with the following levels or return to the previous books before continuing to our advanced curriculum.

By realizing that some topics of the introductory levels of the School of Life did not cover the needed curriculum for holistic health seekers who want to help others restore their health, I decided to prepare a self-healing guide for therapists in the next advanced level of the 200 series to complete the requirements to pass the final exam of our lives. This gave rise to *Spirituality 201: Discovering the Inner Healer: A Self-Healing Manual for Therapists*.

In *Spirituality 201*, I focus my educational effort on how all therapists with varied therapeutic styles can be more effective with their healing techniques without leaving their current field of expertise. This book directs its energy toward the refinement of how the healer's intention and the patient's perception, blended, are the key to success. It will also discuss how the therapist's intention supports the placebo effect and the patient's faith. Concepts already addressed in other books, such as the law of cause and effect and the karma of the patient and healer, will be included. It will also review individual and collective experiences of illness and how inheritance influences the healing process. It also introduces my new view of medicine, which I call holographic medicine, a larger perspective on disease that includes all components of the holographic universe.

In the second book of the postgraduate series, *Spirituality 202*, we try to integrate all the knowledge obtained in our journey by digging into the deepest causal roots of the matter-antimatter relationship of our universal hologram. That can result in unbalanced processes that we perceive as diseases in the biological reality we know as life. We explain in a simple format the complex skein of epigenetic science and how the lifestyles of our ancestors influenced the current state of our genome through mutations in their genetic programs.

Similar to all my books, new readers should be aware that these attempts to guide the reader in the self-discovery of the inner truth that resides in each person avoid giving "patented" healing prescriptions or treasure maps that will assure the reader of their happiness and well-being. This involves a degree of individual introspection of the material by the reader that will help each one progress at their own pace according to their effort. Reading *Spirituality 202* can help the most evolved readers, but many will have to read the texts of the previous trilogy—*Spirituality 101*, *103*, and *104*—to assimilate the material better. The benefits of what is learned in this book are not limited to the therapist but are inclusive to the patient, who is considered a causal ally in the learning experience that is the disease.

As we traditionally do, we will have homework questions and exercises after each chapter to develop the skills necessary to understand the message entirely. My inclusive intention will always accompany you through your reading. It will help you *awaken* from the illusion of suffering and sickness in your lives and understand your good or bad experiences as part of the message of individual learning. In this manner, we can appreciate how inclusive or exclusive intentions hold us accountable for these results. Welcome to this journey of self-healing.

CHAPTER 1

In the Beginning, after the Great Explosion of Love, the Universe Always Sought Harmony in the Disequilibrating Equilibrium of Its Parts

As we discussed at the beginning of several of my books, in the dormant state of the previous multiverse, there was only the unaware emptiness of being, like the canvas waiting for the creative explosion of the painter's brush.

The explosion, or big bang, that awakens the multiverse from its sleep causes the first creative imbalance of consciousness by dividing the energy of the universe's singularity into two parts. This separation creates for the first time an unevenness that produces the first balancing reaction of yin energy that seeks reunification with its opposite, the yang energy. From this unbalanced process of the perception of duality, the consciousness of self, memory, and time is born.

The balancing response of the fragments yearning to become one again creates another imbalance. That gives rise to the third part of the creation triangle: the offspring resulting from the reconnection of the yin and yang that gives rise to the tai chi symbol. This represents the unbalanced generative quality of the universe, which will lead it continuously, subsequently, in the creative or changing process of the new multiverse.

TAI CHI AS AN ARCHETYPAL SYMBOL OF UNIVERSAL BALANCE

This symbol is an archetype of the contrasting dual nature of all actions in the universe, manifested in opposing forces and recurrent cycles. The dark represents the lack of light, the cold, the feminine, the passive, and the centripetal, which binds, attracts, and collects. The white represents the light, the hot, the masculine, the active, and the centrifugal, which separates, repels, and sows. The colored spheres on its opposite symbolize that the opposite is always potentially within its counterpart, ready to manifest itself according to the cycle.

This archetype can contain a potential immensity of ideas, such as motherhood, paternity, climate cycles, chemical and physical reactions, agricultural production cycles, physiological processes of biological organisms, mental creativity, etc. If we understand everything abstracted in this archetype, we can create new and infinite ideas for our material experience.

UNBALANCE AS THE CHANGING NATURAL STATE OF THE UNIVERSAL HOLOGRAM

Our universe is in a continuous state of imbalance and re-equilibration, which, thanks to our subjective perception, freezes the continuity of time like still portraits that we keep in our memory—like a film we project with the camera of our mind. This happens at a speed that divides the timeless instantaneous experience into a relative temporal perception of the past, present, and future.

The attachment of the mind to maintain everything in order (balance) generates the emotions that originate the pleasant and unpleasant feelings and the toil that arises from the effort to ensure the order that guarantees these pleasurable feelings. This suggests that suffering is a creative illusion of the emotional attachment of the mind when resisting the natural state of the continuously changing universal equilibrium; therefore the opposite circumstances of happiness and suffering and health and disease are only situations of balance and imbalance, where the universal hologram never selects one preferentially. We should remember that the law of cause and effect applies to the balancing process so that the intensity of the result will occur proportionately to the initial precipitating cause.

As I will discuss in other chapters, the toxicity that affects the equilibrium of the universal hologram and its components (us) is created by the mesh's disruption of the love intertwined by the (we) principle and weakened by the disconnectedness of the (me) focus of the ego, the source of our emotions. This will trap our consciousness in the restrictive tridimensional space of time within the timeless reality of our majestic holographic experience. Simply put, the spiritual consciousness (antimatter) feels trapped within the physical consciousness (matter) within time and space. This will give rise to the emotional kaleidoscope of contrasting pleasant and unpleasant experiences that will drive many of us to seek the pleasant ones and avoid the disagreeable ones. This attachment to the enjoyable ones will give rise to the human experience of suffering since time and entropy will ensure a continuous change in the conditions we are attached to.

The potential of being able to observe both balance and imbalance as natural processes is the source of the wisdom of the masters, who learned to live in the material universe "with their feet on the ground, but their gaze in heaven," and what the Buddha called the philosophy of the Middle Way.

Review Questions

1. In your own words, explain the term *balancing imbalance*.

2. Reflect on moments that happened in that manner.

3. Why does it take time to understand the balancing part of the imbalance?

4. Why do I call the law of karma the law of love in other books?

5. In your experience, try to recall the emotions associated with attachment to unmet desires or goals.

CHAPTER 2

The Empathy of the Universal Experience as a Holographic Multiverse: Imbalances That Awaken the Consciousness of Our Inclusiveness

Imbalances are the alarms that alert the hologram to take the rebalancing actions necessary for our welfare interdependently.

The experiences of suffering that we consider imbalances generate the state of disease, which gradually awakens our inclusive holographic consciousness of "we are" but numbs the individual exclusive consciousness of "me," which separates us from the infinite contrasts of duality. These alert us that every experience of unbalance is interdependent and holographic, not an individual experience. This can awaken our empathy, patience, and understanding by the equilibrating processes of the suffering of other consciousness that share the hologram.

UNBALANCE IS ALWAYS EQUILIBRATING FOR THE HOLOGRAPHIC CONSCIOUSNESS

The balancing imbalance will only be perceived as uneasiness in the hologram when one of its parts breaks the continuity or consciousness of inclusiveness by attaching preferentially to one of the re-equilibrating experiences; however, these preferences in the individual segments of the hologram could be considered beneficial to the well-being and health of that particular part of the hologram. Ironically, they could harm the hologram's total equilibrium.

The attachment to a specific type of an unbalancing equilibrium awakens the experience of exclusiveness that disconnects our holographic consciousness entirely from its inclusiveness, which leaves the person at the mercy of the law of cause and effect, trapped in an imaginary three-dimensional segment of the universe experiencing life as rebirth, disease, and death. This isolation and attachment to our exclusive experiences create a swarm of emotions that give rise to the contrasting illusions of suffering, joy, sickness, and health.

The unknowing exclusive action of any individual part generates more intensity in the equilibrating response of the inclusive hologram, which increases the severity of the perception of suffering and disease in the individual excluded or separated from its original hologram. For example, suppose we imagined our planet as a hologram of our human experience. In that case, the irresponsible actions that individuals or governments make that impact climatic change, which could seem beneficial to a particular geographical region, may negatively impact distant areas. The butterfly effect analyzes these in our planet, suggesting they could generate natural disasters such as earthquakes and hurricanes, affecting remote regions unrelated to the geographical areas that started the climate imbalance. There are no isolated individual regional benefits or natural disasters for the holographic planetary consciousness, but only equilibrating imbalances that seek to harmonize the totality of the planetary hologram.

All equilibrating imbalances for the individual consciousnesses, self-isolated by their independent intention, will appear to be harmful. This occurs in the biological hologram when these manifest themselves as symptoms and diseases, yet are only the alarms in the organism, whose purpose is only to awaken the inclusiveness and well-being of the biological organism. In my clinical experience, I often observe the paradoxical reaction of my patients to severe diseases when in their spiritual maturity, they understand these as balancing love lessons and not as punishments that generate unfair suffering in their lives.

Sickness appears in the three-dimensional material universe when exclusive intention and time generate attachment, and these emotions associate suffering with unbalances we perceive as diseases.

When one of the components of the individual hologram coexists in the three-dimensional experience of space-time matter, this excludes the disagreeable experiences of balancing imbalances. Through its attachment to the balanced (agreeable) ones, it will develop contrasting emotions. This is good when an individual obtains the expected response and harmful when the unexpected ones are experienced. Their preference (attachment) for the state of equilibrium they expect and aversion to the one they reject is the actual cause of their suffering.

In other books, I emphasize that the process of being born, living, aging, and dying is the cause of the progressive inflammatory experience, which deteriorates our organisms and is what we perceive as aging in our lives. This process can occur at variable rhythms, depending on how we use the vitality or energy reserve (longevity) inherited from our parents.

Suppose our dietary, physical, sexual, or emotional lifestyles are unbalanced. Our holograms' excessive energy expenditure to rebalance them can create premature aging associated with diseases (alarms, imbalances) that hinder individuals from regaining their optimal conditions or original well-being. These severely unstable conditions are equivalent to what we know as chronic and degenerative diseases. As postulated in the science of epigenetics, many of these imbalances are recorded in our genomes and passed on to our offspring as states of potential illnesses (mutations) that can manifest according to the quality of lifestyles we maintain.

THE ORIGIN OF THE HOLOGRAPHIC TOXICITY AND ITS RELATIONSHIP TO THE DISEASE PROCESS

The most interdependent and inclusive systems are less toxic than exclusive ones.

This is because conscious life is a continuous (yin) or balancing effort to counteract the force of entropy (yang). It is like observing our beautiful, groomed garden return to its original state of weeds and wild bushes when we go on a holiday. Therefore, based on the law of energy conservation, we should understand that the harmony of the hologram has an energy cost and effort, which will depend on the degree of imbalance or toxicity created by the entropy of the system. It was this expense that we previously described as aging. *We must understand that this toxic state results from our lack of awareness and responsibility regarding our decisions' inclusive or exclusive nature.*

That is why the most interdependent (inclusive) holographic systems will have more resistance to entropy and the more independent (exclusive) more weakness. The tendency to be more prone to entropy disorder is known as toxicity. In the biological realm, it is referred to as inflammation and aging, which present with varying degrees of symptoms and disease. Biologically, this deficiency is manifested in the weakness of our immunological system, which leaves us exposed to internal or external threats to our organism. *This toxicity is the corrective result*, spontaneously generated by the parties' unconscious (selfish) action (cause) on their holographic consciousness that we know as suffering. In the densest (lowest vibrational) planes of the material universe, the biological being lives and dreams in these with the five physical senses of the biological organism, which reinforces the exclusiveness of the individual experience and separates us from the experiences of our fellow travelers in the holographic universe, which would misleadingly appear to be an isolated occurrence of suffering.

The limited realization of the individual having a beginning and an end of the biological experience in time gives rise to the ego and emotions that occur and result from suffering. This hinders our response to the entropy of our organism, ages us (inflames), and shortens the longevity and quality of our life.

THE PURITY OF THE ENERGY SOURCE DETERMINES THE EXTENT OF THE INFLAMMATORY EXPENDITURE TO REBALANCE THE HOLOGRAPHIC TOXICITY

Since the hologram is always looking for the

least costly way (energy use) to maintain its balance, the purest sources of energy and more inclusive actions that generate less toxicity will be preferred.

HOW TO ENSURE THE PURITY OF ENERGY

Where is it most important to guarantee this? We accumulate toxicity in the blueprints of our biological material experience because of our ancestors' legacy and current dietary and mental lifestyles. As mentioned in the science of epigenetics, this process is facilitated by detoxifying the inherited tendencies and preventing future toxicity by ensuring the quality or purity of the energy utilized.

THE UNIVERSE IS A HOLOGRAPHIC EXPERIENCE WITHIN AN IMMEASURABLE HOLOGRAPHIC MULTIVERSE

I have attempted to describe the tendencies to disease in this chapter as holographic alarms spontaneously autogenerated by the universal consciousness to stabilize the experience for the benefit of all its parts. In the following chapters, I will introduce how holographic entanglement spreads to other universes or multiverses. Each universe's components, including our physical components, are multiverses responding to holographic entanglement laws.

Review Questions

1. In our three-dimensional earthly experience, why is it almost inevitable to develop an exclusive intention?

2. Why is it easier to awaken inclusive intention when we view the holographic experience as multidimensional?

3. How do linear time, memory, attachment, and suffering foster exclusive intention?

4. Is exclusive action always unnecessary?

5. What is the origin of the toxicity accumulated by the individual hologram?

6. Review how the physical law of entanglement supports the holographic nature of our universe and how love is the way we perceive it as individuals.

CHAPTER 3

A Holographic Vision of
Health and Disease

THE HOLOGRAPHIC MEDICINE MODEL

Within the context of the holographic model that supports the new science of epigenetics, I want to introduce a fresh vision of the origin of health and disease. I will demonstrate that this new scheme inclusively fits any previously postulated model of the causes of diseases and will facilitate more preventive and comprehensive management of these. This model will describe the sequence of imbalances in the time continuum within its biological, mental-emotional, and spiritual components, including how these changes influence the universal hologram interdependently and how they are recorded in our organic system, the genome. This model will also explain how the epigenetic influence of both harmful and beneficial lifestyles can perpetuate or prevent diseases.

We must be clear that the law of cause and effect always steers the entire holographic system and its components in inclusive and specific responses to the imbalance created in the hologram, which will be the equivalent of the alarms of the organism to correct the inequality before irreparable damage occurs. *As discussed in previous chapters, these alarms are guided by the law of causality (love), triggered by the inclusiveness or exclusiveness of the intention and resulting action*. One can later understand that silencing the alarms (symptoms), as modern pharmaceutical medicine does, is not a comprehensive or inclusive way to accomplish this.

THE ESSENTIAL FEATURES OF THE MODEL

A hologram is a three-dimensional projection created from a flat image using the uniformity of laser light. The main feature of this projection is that it can be replicated in its entirety from any part of the hologram without considering its original size.

Etymological origin: "Holo," which means complete or whole.

Gram: Record, write, or describe the total that manifests itself in its parts.

Dr. Bhom, a theoretical physicist, postulated a holographic theory on the mind-matter relationship, where universal creation could be explained by the coherent relationship of its parts within the holographic particularity of the universe. It was based on observing the coherence or interdependence between the elements of a hologram, which suggested that all its components were intertwined in some relationship without apparent physical continuity.

This relationship was then verified by the theoretical physics law of quantum entanglement.

The model posits that the human being and its travel companions are individual holograms within the universal scheme, which respond to each other in interdependent inclusivity, like that described in the phenomenon of quantum entanglement. This will result in specific effects for the participating human holograms, depending on their individual experience and wisdom accumulated by their intentions of using their "free will."

ESSENTIAL PRINCIPLES OF THE HOLOGRAPHIC THEORY OF DISEASE

- It is integrative, coherent, and intertwined in its origin, manifestations (disease), and correction (treatment). A harmonious and inescapable correlation exists between the imbalance and its corrective response.
- It has its start and resolution time; therefore each imbalance has its beginning and end in proportion to its impact on the holographic balance.

- The process of sickness (unbalance) is archived within the holographic experience; this information is recorded and transmitted from generation to generation in our genomes. It is the correction of this imbalance that heals the disease both in the biological organism and genome.

HOLOGRAPHIC HEALTH

Before heeding its individual component's needs, the hologram will always focus on the entire universe's interdependent balance (health).

- The universal hologram focuses on its general well-being above the individual parts and allows for regional disharmonic processes that balance the total experience. These are the symptoms that cause us so much discomfort. The climatic effects of our planet are strong examples of this.

- The primary purpose of symptoms is to alert the hologram and seek correction of the root cause of the imbalance, similar to the concept of love lessons to explain the suffering in our lives that I described in my book, *The Forgiveness Code*.

- The corrective effect focuses more on the progressive sequence of imbalances that primarily affect the hologram's total interdependence than its components. Even if it has several simultaneous symptoms, our organism can only focus on the most prominent and only recognize the less noticeable after correcting the more obvious ones. So the resolution and appearance occur in levels, or layers, as when peeling an onion.

THE SACRED GEOMETRY OF THE HOLOGRAPHIC UNIVERSE LIES WITHIN THE CIRCLES OF CONSCIOUSNESS THAT CREATE ITS INTERDEPENDENCY

As we discover new aspects of universal laws, I have always maintained that knowledge is like progressive, inclusive concentric circles that expand their diameters yet include the previous circle's data. As a result, no learning experience should be discarded since it can be used when the opportunity comes. That is why wisdom grows with our mistakes and not only by our successes.

The quantum entanglement more thoroughly highlights this dynamic than all previous philosophical phrases, such as "as above, so below." This encompasses a macro-and microperspective of physics.

At present, the limitations of science and its instruments still need to unify all theoretical physics laws that could explain our universe's interdependent holographic relationship. Questions still unanswered include: Does the universe have a beginning and an end point? What existed before the big bang? How do scientific laws view the existence of our consciousness in a postulated multidimensional universe? Do multiverses exist? How can we reconcile these possibilities with traditional religious beliefs? I will attempt to dwell on these questions in my next book, *Healing the Cancer in Our Genes*.

A HOLOGRAPHIC MODEL OF THE UNIVERSE

Let us start from the microcosm and ease ourselves into the macrocosm:

Matter—elementary particles and atoms—elements—chemical-organic compounds—biologic organisms—planet Earth—solar system—Milky Way galaxy—Virgo Cluster galaxy—supercluster galaxies (ten million of these are in the universe)—our universe—our multiverse within infinite other multiverses. As you can observe, this is a never-ending story with a very entertaining plot that will never bore you, just like this book.

Antimatter: This invisible, undefinable portion is calculated to occupy 96 percent of our universe. In my previous books, I refer to it as our source of origin—the spirit or the undefinable emptiness that existed before the big bang.

Reviewing our microcosmic and macrocosmic chain of manifestations in matter, we must understand that holographic interdependence exists in all its infinite components. So our universe is a timeless spiral of ascending and descending concentric circles that meet at their points of convergence and interdependence. These converging points create the spiral motions of multidimensional experiences of time. If you look at a spiral staircase from above or below, it will seem like a circle.

ILLNESS: SEEKING THE BALANCE OF THE HOLOGRAM

The appearance of symptoms and diseases in our holograms will depend on corrupt programs or mutations in our biological DNA.

This activation occurs through the introduction of toxic mental or alimentary experiences. Mutations in our genomes are activated by a wide range of toxicity caused by poor eating or mental lifestyles.

The severity of the imbalance or disease will depend on the severity of the mutation, its duration in the genome, and the emotional reaction of the biological being to the symptoms. As a result, older alterations will take longer to detox.

The key to our holographic well-being is purifying our genomes by detoxifying our body from harmful mutations and activating our stored good mutations by supplying the purest materials.

The longer the negative change in the genome has lasted, the longer it will take to deactivate it.

Thus, the secret to holographic well-being lies in detoxifying (rebalancing) our genomes by detoxifying (rebalancing) our organisms, facilitating our good mutations by providing the purest raw materials.

If we persist in this process, we will bring our biological DNA to its optimal state to ensure the holographic health of our off-spring for generations to come.

FINAL PURPOSE OF THE EVOLUTIONARY HOLOGRAPHIC PROCESS

If we continue this detoxifying process, we can purify ourselves until we reach the optimal holographic balance of our biological DNA. Then only the best mutations will be passed on to the next generation.

ORIGIN OF HOLOGRAPHIC DISEASE: HEREDITARY OR ACQUIRED ORIGIN

Inherited diseases are not only transmitted by modern mendelian hereditary laws that don't include family tendencies to suffer more often customary conditions, such as asthma, arthritis, autoimmune, bipolarity, depression, and cancer.

The penetration of these diseases into one of its family members will depend on the good or bad epigenetic effects promoted by the quality of the current individual lifestyle.

A conundrum of treatment is created by the diverging views of the disease process, as discussed in our theory of holographic medicine.

Holographic medicine emphasizes that without treating the roots in the disease process, as it occurs in plants, the condition will recur and not heal. Except for treating infectious diseases, modern medicine has focused its efforts on the branches or symptoms of the disease and not on its causes. This emphasis on eradicating the symptoms rapidly has developed a complex, costly pharmaceutical industry that has been very efficient in treating the symptoms, which are the warning signs of the pathological process, but have minimal effects on eradicating or healing the cause at its root.

This has allowed disease progression into severe degenerative conditions and cancer by not eradicating the primary causes. Paradoxically, this created a medical system that promotes the persistence of the disease process to ensure its economic survival.

ACQUIRED HOLOGRAPHIC DISEASE: THE EMOTIONAL CONNECTION

Acquired diseases are usually the result of the combined effect of dietary and emotional toxicities. But in my experience, the emotional component is the most influential. The most potent emotional toxin that precipitates the process is *guilt*, which is repressed in deep areas of our subconscious mind, where the experience is imprisoned in a repetitive cycle, along with the historical person who lived it at the time of the occurrence. This is discussed further in *The Forgiveness Code*.

The shame and suffering associated with the memory of the event lead us to suppress the memory of the event altogether.

This person feels abandoned in the person's subconscious within their experience at that time. This encourages the imprisoned party to call out to the incarcerated person through their autonomic nervous system using symptoms such as panic attacks, nightmares, guilt, depression, endocrine disorders, digestive disorders, and aches.

Forgiveness and empathy arising from the awareness of our inclusive, love-sustained holographic existence is the most effective remedy for healing guilt.

In my practice, we help the patient locate the repressed events and use the forgiveness code to free the incarcerated person and bring them to the actual reality in its present. As we reprogram their toxic lifestyles while integrating the forgiveness code, most of their symptoms disappear, and a more hopeful vision of life is reborn in them. In my book *The Forgiveness Code*, I compare our organism's diseases or injuries to self-inflicted wounds sustained in inner battles between warriors of the light (spirit) and of their shadows (ego's ignorance).

Other techniques are available for therapists to release these repressed emotions, but my preference is to promote self-release by the patient.

THE SELF-INFLICTED INJURIES GENERATED BY STRESS CAN BE THE CAUSE OF DISEASE

A proper balance between the sympathetic and parasympathetic nervous systems ensures the appropriate response of the cardiovascular, gastrointestinal, endocrine (glandular), and immunological systems, which are essential for the survival of our organism. Recent studies have shown its harmful effects on the immune system and clinical depression.[1] Other studies have shown that chronic stress exposure can affect executives' cognitive functionality.[2] Effects of hyperactivity in the sympathetic system can create heart irregularity and hypertension.[3] An increase in heart attack rates has been reported during traffic rush hours.[4] Since the autonomic system is connected to all the major organs, any dysfunction can precipitate alterations in those affected organs.

Our gastrointestinal system is a frequent scapegoat for emotional disharmonies, which can respond with bloating, indigestion, heartburn, diarrhea, and constipation. As discussed in this section, the repeated stress response can weaken our emergency response to a life-or-death crisis.

In this section, I would like to delve more extensively into the stress response of the human organism and attempt to answer the following questions: What exactly is its purpose? How does our organism mediate it? What are the various stages of the response? How do we recognize its effects on our bodies? How can we adapt to its impact without damaging effects on our organs?

THE RELATIONSHIP OF STRESS AND EMOTIONS IN ILLNESS

This is the physiological mechanism that the body has evolved to adapt and survive within its external and internal environment. This adaptation mechanism involves the everyday use and wear and tear of our body due to its adaptation (aging).

From birth, the human being is exposed to stress after having minimal effects in the mother's womb, such as its first breath, crying, exposure to extreme temperatures, and the need to ingest nutrients to survive and eliminate accumulated toxins.

It is not just tension in our nervous system; it is all the tension that occurs in all body parts and all its systems.

It is neither bad nor good, such as our first loving kiss, sex, competitive sports, or our first solo drive.

This response is controlled by an interaction between the nervous, endocrine, and immune systems, in which a complex release of hormones and neuropeptides prepares the body to defend its integrity. The table below outlines the reactions to how our system responds to stress.

GENERAL RESPONSES OF OUR SYSTEM TO THE STRESS RESPONSE
Pupillary dilation
Increased metabolism and temperature
Increased heart rate and strength
Increased blood pressure
Increased breathing rate
Increased arterial circulation to the brain, heart, and muscles

The adaptation response consists of three parts:

A. the alarm reaction

B. stage of resistance

C. stage of exhaustion (wear and tear)

ALARM RESPONSE AND MAINTENANCE

These two are the ones that generally occur in healthy people.

The alarm activates the process when it is exposed to a harmful or life-threatening situation. The system then goes into a state of alert for any eventuality.

EXHAUSTION STAGE

If, for repeated causes, we activate and keep the system on alert excessively, it can collapse. The body warns us of potential collapse by presenting physical or mental symptoms, such as frequent infectious diseases, insomnia, extreme tiredness, digestive disorders, high blood pressure, depression, sadness, addiction, and loss of libido.

The typical response becomes problematic when the individual interpretation of danger activates the response falsely, leading to exhaustion.

The adaptive response began in primitive humans and animals to adapt and survive in a hostile environment under the constant threat of death.

The basis of the exhaustion stage originates in the subjective interpretation of immediate danger to the individual, which in our divergent modern lifestyles and upbringings has created an exaggeration of fears within the usual challenges that occur within educational, professional, and familial experiences.

GREAT EXPECTATIONS GIVE BIRTH TO GREAT FRUSTRATIONS

The expectations of others and ourselves and the lack of self-awareness of our capabilities lead us to repeat bouts of frustration and anger, ending in abysmal self-esteem. These frustrating experiences repeatedly activate the stress mechanism until our system collapses.

We must realize that neurohormonal activation takes twenty-four hours to deactivate, implying that the effects on the body will be prolonged after the precipitating event.

SIGNS THAT INDICATE WE ARE DRAINING THE SYSTEM	
Chest tightness and palpitations	Oral and throat dryness
Lack of clarity and mental focus	Impulsive behavior and emotional instability
Physical and mental fatigue	Unfounded fears
Exaggerated sweating	Irritation with loud noises and lights
Insomnia	Digestive disturbances
Period pain and irregularity	Neck and back pain and spasms

Altered appetite	Addictions
Physiological effects of prolonged adaptation response	Increased or decreased thyroid hormone levels
Decreased testosterone levels	Increased prolactin levels
Decreased normal LH response and ovulation	Increased blood glucose levels
Altered circadian rhythm via the pineal gland	

EXPERIMENTAL EVIDENCE OF EFFECTS ON THE IMMUNE SYSTEM
Decreased antibody response
Decreased rejection of skin grafts
Development of autoimmune diseases in animals (rheumatoid arthritis)
Increased tumor growth in animals

DISEASES RELATED TO PROLONGED STRESS	
Peptic ulcers	Ulcerative colitis and Crohn's disease
Spastic colon	Interstitial cystitis
Essential hypertension	Heart attacks

Autoimmune diseases	Hyperthyroidism
Bronchial asthma	Depression
Cancer	

WHY THE INDIVIDUAL VARIABILITY IN RESPONSE AND SYMPTOM DEVELOPMENT?

It is known that the body's response can be more intense in specific organs or systems.

It is postulated that this depends on heredity traits and lifestyles, such as nutrition, work environment, sex, age, education, and economic situation.

UNHAPPINESS AND ATTACHMENT: THE EMOTIONAL LINK TO ORIGINS OF STRESS

The unceasing search for happiness focuses

on material goods. Recognition and prestige based on the laws of the world create perennial dissatisfaction, especially when confronted with the reality that it is impossible to be happy all the time. This pushes us toward the insatiable vortex of the search for pleasure. I will discuss the link between emotions and disease in other sections of this book. Meditation as an effective tool to recommunicate with our source or creator will also be addressed in another segment. The reason for our breakage in communication with our inner source or guide is the tendency not to listen to God in our prayers.

Remember: Meditation helps us hear the answer to our prayers. Praying is talking to God. Meditation is listening to God.

HEALING TECHNIQUES FOR OUR EMOTIONAL WOUNDS

The problem with healing emotional wounds

is that since they originate from mental causes, they do not respond effectively to physical-based therapies, so they need spiritual and cognitive approaches to heal. These emotional wounds fester until all infectious emotional pathogens are eliminated.

You can find information about these methods, which we shall mention without detailed explanations in the media. They all stem from the concept that emotions are stored with their harmful code, adversely influencing physical welfare and presenting physical symptoms.

1. Traditional psychology: Follows the fundamental principles established in academic psychology.

2. Transpersonal psychology: A therapeutic approach aimed at having human beings achieve optimal levels of welfare and psychological help,

highlighting modifications of states of awareness beyond the limits of ego and personality. It connects psychology with spirituality, seeking humanity's self-realization and self-transcendence.

3. *Ho'oponopono*: This is a very ancient Hawaiian art of conflict resolution based on reconciliation and forgiveness. The original Hawaiians, the islands' first inhabitants, used to practice it. Morrnah Nalamaku Simeona (May 19, 1913–February 11, 1992) brought and updated these teachings for modern times. Today they are used by practitioners and therapists across different disciplines.

THERAPIES TO UNLOAD EMOTIONS

1. Neurolinguistic programming (NLP): NLP is a model for how our mind

works, how this affects language, and how to use this knowledge to program ourselves in the sense of making our lives and the things we do easier and more efficient at the same time. Though most practitioners are psychologists, studying it is not a prerequisite. It has several variants to discharge and heal emotions.

2. Clinical hypnosis: Practiced by physicians, nonphysicians, and psychologists, it can be used to heal past emotional wounds.

3. Hypnotic regression therapy: Though it is used to treat emotional experiences that allegedly originate in past lives, some use it for regressions in this life.

4. Somato Emotional Release: This is a therapeutic variant of craniosacral therapies that help rid the mind and

body of the residual effects of past trauma associated with negative experiences. Joint research efforts by Dr. John Upledger and biophysicist Dr. Zvi Karni led to the discovery that the body often conserves physical forces rather than dissipates them, and it often saves the accompanying emotional energy unleashed by a physiological, psychological, emotional, or spiritual trauma. As the body heals, you can isolate or separate this energy into an "energy cyst." Though a body can initially adapt to the presence of this "energy cyst," it finally weakens or gets tired of hosting it. As a result, pain, dysfunction, or emotional stress may develop.

5. Craniosacral therapy: Controversial field developed from traditional osteopathic medicine by Dr. John Upledger.

Medical and nonmedical professionals can practice this.

6. Traditional Chinese acupuncture: My favorite, since it is part of my acupuncture practice, in which emotions affect specific organs that project as organic diseases in the body. Rebalancing the organ involves removing the associated symptom.

7. Applied kinesiology (Touch for Health): Touch for Health is a holistic method derived from the clinical practice of applied kinesiology. It allows activating the patient's resources to recover their health with straightforward and efficient techniques. Dr. John Thie created it based on the acupuncture meridians and divided it into four levels (I–IV) to initiate us into the knowledge of applied kinesiology. This system

emphasizes the beginning of recovering health, initially reestablishing structural balance, as it is impossible to experience optimal health if the body and muscles are unbalanced. This dynamic acknowledges that human beings possess various aspects—physical, biochemical, emotional, intellectual, and spiritual—and that all require balancing.

8. Finger tapping and eye movement release: Remarkably effective alternative that can be self-applied for an emotional release that has proven effective in veterans with PTSD.

These emotional alterations acquired in our DNA are the easiest to reverse and prevent from happening in future generations. Like many other authors, I believe toxic emotions are one of the primary factors in activating precancerous mutations in our genomes.

Review Questions

1. How can you link emotions to physical and mental illness?

2. How could these create a mutation in our genomes? Are all these harmful to the organism?

3. How can we inhibit harmful emotions and promote beneficial emotions?

4. What factors contribute to disease severity and duration (unbalance) in the body?

CHAPTER 4

The Importance of Bioethical Philosophy in the Practice of the Holistic Therapist

OUR UNIVERSE VISUALIZED AS A BEING OR HOLOGRAPHIC CONSCIOUSNESS

Our universe is a conscious holographic being governed by the law of cause and effect (law of love), which equally holds accountable each of the individual holograms that populate it. Its evolutionary purpose is to obtain the functional harmony of all its parts to manifest in interdependence all the creative potential in the most inclusive form to benefit all aspects of the hologram. This was the purpose of creating the human being in the most subtle dimensions, where human consciousness was placed in a dreamlike state of innocence, in the account of the Garden of Eden, where its consciousness should awaken to direct the discovery of the immense reality potentially residing within the Great Dream of the Great Explosion (big bang) of Love.

The lifestyle that harmoniously includes all the components of our three-dimensional biological experience is the bioethical lifestyle. In the next section, I will describe its characteristics in medicine.

HOW DOES THE INDIVIDUAL PART OF THE HOLOGRAM BECOME DISCONNECTED FROM ITS SOURCE? WHAT FACTORS PROMOTE THE PROCESS?

To understand this, we should realize that all the parts of the universal hologram must have a single language that interdependently interconnects them after the appearance of duality occurred after the big bang. The universe appeared in infinite manifestations of time and space, which forced its need to maintain communication between its parts. That originated all the countless languages that developed after the initial expansion. This resulted in progressive communication disruptions between its components, especially among the spirit (antimatter) and physical (matter). This creates an apparent feeling of isolation for the biological experience from its origins, which then is forced to develop the ego as its source, which will be directed to remember its true origins by the law of cause and effect and the emotional realm of disease and suffering.

The final solution is to remember our origins and universal language by reconnecting to our spiritual (antimatter) origins. To understand our forgotten universal language, we must remember that its alphabet is composed of the letters of love. Paradoxically, the experience of suffering and self-forgiveness awakens empathy and love in our holographic memory. As I mentioned in my book *The Forgiveness Code*, there are many techniques to accomplish this, but in this one, I will only review the reconnection techniques of meditation.

MEDITATION

Meditation is a self-directed technique in which we focus our mental processes, internally or externally, to establish a state of physical and mental relaxation that calms all thought activity. This state fosters pleasant, harmonious, and precise physiological effects in the body.

It complements the benefits of traditional prayers and other forms of verbal communication with our source, similar to wire-based connections.

Yet meditation is more of a wireless communication in which, after typing our needs and grievances, we wait quietly for the response of the "person" on the other side. And even when we must cut our present connection, we can receive unceasing responses from the other side by following our previous thread. The source never disconnects from us, even if we forget to return to our original thread.

For the scientifically documented benefits of meditation, please refer to the tenth chapter of my book *The Forgiveness Code*.

MEDITATION: PREPARATION AND PREREQUISITES

1. The proper attitude
2. The proper place
3. The proper time
4. The proper technique(s)

THE PROPER ATTITUDE

This must be based on the interdependence with other living beings and must show:

1. Wisdom—knowledge and understanding
2. Humility

3. Creative, loving, and unselfish intention

4. Respect—all beings have their potential light

5. Patience—without temporal demands or expectations, each person progresses at their own pace.

These are the attributes intrinsic to the warrior of light.

THE PROPER PLACE

The setting must have the characteristics that foster the appropriate calmness in body and mind:

1. Physical safety and privacy

2. Pleasant temperature

3. Pollution-free atmosphere and air

4. Noise-free

5. Open natural spaces—mountains, near lakes, seas, and forests

It is evident that, in our modern lives, we cannot easily access places with all the previous characteristics, but we can set a private location in our home and give it our distinctive touch.

THE PROPER TIME

The usual recommendation is early in the morning, when the mind and body are more rested, but it is okay at night for those who feel better at that time of day. Initially, we must begin with short periods of five to ten minutes or for the time we can manage without the body and mind making a fuss. You will see that, with more experience, meditating for half an hour becomes easy.

The ideal frequency would be to get better daily results.

THE PROPER TECHNIQUE—POSTURE

According to all Asian traditions, the body and the mind mirror are interrelated through an endless web of energy channels, concentrated in some body areas as energy centers or chakras. This energy network must flow harmoniously for our body to work and for the mind and body to communicate effectively. The physical body's correct posture is essential to carry its circulation appropriately.

Though there are many variants, we shall discuss the seven points of posture recommended by the Buddha Vairocana.

1. Cross your legs in a half lotus or full lotus.

2. Place your hands on your lap, fingers interlocked, right hand over your left hand, with your thumbs slightly touching. An alternative is to place your palms on your knees.

3. Your spinal column must be perfectly vertical.

4. Your elbows should not touch the sides of your body. To achieve this effect, you must lift your shoulders slightly.

5. Your head is slightly bowed forward, but your neck aligns with your spinal column.

6. As for your mouth, your jaw is relaxed and slightly open, and your tongue contacts your palate.

7. Your eyes are kept partially open, focusing on your nose or thirty degrees to the front or toward the floor. If they

close naturally, it is all right if we do not squint.

MODIFICATION OF THE SITTING POSTURE

Older adults, people with physical limitations, or those with disabilities may meditate sitting down if they observe the previous requirements, particularly regarding the back. They must not lean on the backrest.

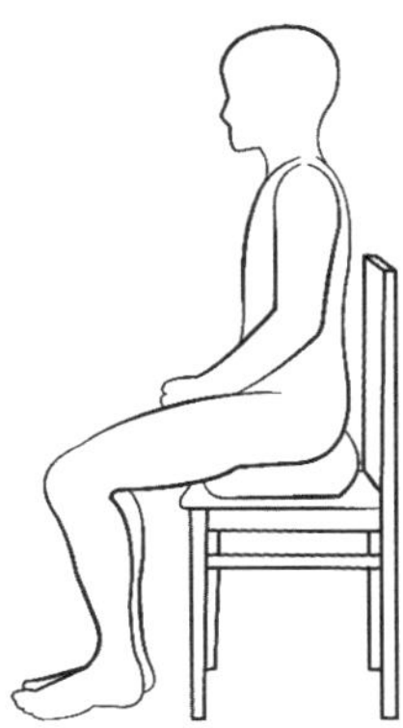

THE TECHNIQUE—SUMMARY

Preparation

1. Body relaxation (appropriate position and attitude, slight stretching, visualization of a pleasant moment)

2. Creating the mental space (developing the feeling of protection with a circle of love)

3. Concentration—focusing our mind (*Shamata*)

4. Freeing the mind and allowing it to fuse with its origins (silence, space, emptiness) (*Vipassana*)

5. Reintegration into our material reality

6. Merit dedication (giving thanks and sharing)

THE TWO TIBETAN BUDDHIST MEDITATION TECHNIQUES: *SHAMATA* AND *VIPASSANA*

SHAMATA (CONCENTRATION)

At first, the mind behaves like a wild monkey that jumps ceaselessly from branch to branch. The most efficient way to calm the mind is to focus it on external or internal objects.

EXTERNAL *SHAMATA*

In this technique, we focus our attention on objects with a pleasant meaning, such as:

Sacred or religious objects

A lit candle

INTERNAL *SHAMATA*

In this technique, our concentration is on our breathing.

When we observe it, we must ensure we do not force it and that when we inhale we allow the abdomen to expand to allow maximum airflow to our lungs.

Exhalation usually should be considered to take longer than inhalation (twice as long).

In this technique, the intention or effort is to calm the mind, and we must practice it until we feel comfortable, for at least fifteen minutes.

After mastering this technique, we can go on to the next, *Vipassana*, in which we make no effort. A frequently used method focuses on the expiratory and inspiratory phases of breathing.

VIPASSANA (EFFORTLESS MEDITATION)

In this technique, when we have learned to calm or focus the mind, we observe it and let it loose without restricting it. The goal is to follow the nature of its ceaseless activity, entirely independent of the observer. We must visualize thoughts as clouds drifting in the sky, but they are not the sky. Our true transcendental mind, like a magical mirror, corresponds to a clear sky, yet if we focus on the clouds, we will not be aware of the vastness of the sky, which symbolizes our minds.

Many positive, negative, calming, or exciting thoughts will come, but we must let all of them go by without judging them as good or bad.

When we discover ourselves following each thought (clouds) anew, we must refocus our mind on breathing until it calms, then let go again.

MEASURES TO SUPPORT MEDITATION

During the initial stages, some people will need aids to relax their minds, such as:

1. Incense
2. Music—mantras
3. Altars and religious figures
4. Darkness

Each person will do that which is most comfortable for them.

MEDITATION COMPLEMENTARY TECHNIQUES

1. Visualization
2. Analytical contemplation
3. Mindfulness in action—awareness

VISUALIZATION

1. Visualization is based on the concept that we, sharing a heritage in which this universe originates, can be cocreators of our future reality by visualizing it in our mirror mind.

2. The connection between past, present, and future—we can break the time barrier and create it all three times during the visualization (see the meditation visualization of the warrior of light in the final section of this book).

3. This technique has been a part of the training of great athletes and musical artists in our world.

4. We could compare it to the creation of a tridimensional painting or movie, where we would appear as real as we look in our daily lives.

5. It is an imaginary creation in our mirror mind, which we release through the spaces between the dimensions, making it easy to manifest that visualized reality in our material world.

ANALYTICAL CONTEMPLATION

1. The method used by many Asian schools to analytically understand the reasons behind the structure and origin of our universe within the parameters of logic and reason. It is a method that combines the material world with the spiritual world using reason.

2. All the variable Asian philosophical views arise from it.

MINDFULNESS IN ACTION—AWARENESS

1. Mindfulness is based on the capacity to carry the mental awareness of the meditative state over to everyday activities.

2. It initially depends on trying to observe ourselves or paying more attention to our daily actions and intentions and their effects on others.

3. It is a state of readiness, like observing our mind during a sitting meditation, where we watch it without judging but remain aware of the motivations and outcomes of our actions upon others.

4. This allows us to avoid inappropriate actions and not repeat them.

5. In time, our actions will be more spontaneous and natural, without the need to control our minds.

SELF-ESTEEM AND GUILT

1. One of the many effects of meditation upon the mind is the capacity to improve our self-esteem and pacify our sense of guilt gradually.

2. Depending on our experience during conflict and the purity of the images visualized in our mirror minds, we will all have fears, phobias, and guilt, like emotional battlefield scars.

3. Meditation allows us to understand the truth that:

    » We all originate in the luminous world of the Mirror of our minds.

- » We all possess the light, or the potential, to manifest the attributes of this energy. In time, meditation will help us acknowledge it in ourselves and others and display it in our lives.

4. If we review the material covered, we will see that these shadows were created in our minds by the distortions in our mirror, created in turn by our emotions.

5. We must realize that due to the holographic link of our matrix of light we are all interdependent, and we must share the merit of both the good and the terrible things we have done. *We are co-responsible for our mistakes but not guilty of them*.

6. *Not knowing* that we possess these luminous attributes gives rise to selfish

actions, which may create suffering for ourselves and others. As stated in one of my previous books: "There are no bad people. There are only those who do not yet know their goodness."

All we have shared with you in this chapter was directed to help you develop the vision of disease that will help you create a bioethical view that will support your efforts to guide your patients to their holographic wellness. Let us see what these characteristics are.

CHARACTERISTICS OF THE BIOETHICAL VISION OF MEDICINE THAT THE THERAPIST SHOULD MAINTAIN

1. There are no diseases without the sick patient. That is why we cannot treat the disease without the patient.

2. Diseases result from our ignorance in caring for and preventing imbalances that hold us responsible for the warnings or alarms that the body produces, which we call symptoms and diseases.

3. All the memories of how imbalances were caused are archived in the biological records or DNA memory of each cell in the body.

4. What enters our body by any of the five senses that the body does not recognize as beneficial is considered toxic and will react immunologically to protect itself through the inflammatory process.

5. In its initial stages, the inflammatory process triggers alarms known as symptoms, which can be initially corrected easily. But if these causes are not fixed, the inflammatory process

will progress to more advanced stages of toxicity that we call diseases.

6. Part of the toxic inflammatory process created by our ancestors makes us prone to certain diseases more than others, depending on the toxicity of our lifestyles, as the science of epigenetics has shown us.

7. Most modern therapies in medicine focus on eliminating symptoms (curing), but it does not focus on eliminating the cause (healing) of the disease. That is why therapies that treat symptoms do not permanently resolve them; they will recur and allow toxicity to progress to more severe disorders.

8. The worst toxicity is due to the *mental* effect of emotions stored in the subconscious (past) part of our minds as

guilt, from which we subtly self-inflict our worst diseases. It is in this that the forgiveness code has the best results.

9. The most effective healing process is the detoxification of all accumulated physical and mental toxicities and reversing of the initial process that caused the intoxication.

10. This previous process, to be effective, must be carried out by the person who caused it and cannot be healed by any earthly or spiritual therapeutics guided by third parties.

11. Faith, in remembering our light source, facilitates the process by reconnecting the Son of Man (body) with the Son of God (spirit). Still, we must realize that without the effort to learn the lesson of love hidden within the suffering of the

disease and accept responsibility for its creation, healing will not occur.

12. The above helps us eliminate the feeling of blaming others for our suffering, which portrays us as innocent victims of an unfair destiny. Even inherited imbalances can be corrected by the new science of epigenetics, which allows us to remove the toxic effects from our genome.

When people remember their origins as a child of light, they begin to see every experience of suffering as lessons of love, where they understand the following phrase as it applies to them: "For the best students, God offers the most difficult tests." This makes them allies of light and love to help purify the toxicity (sins) committed by their ancestors when "they did not know what they were doing."

This type of bioethical style of coexistence is what science now knows as epigenetics and is the most preventive and therapeutic weapon to correct defects in our genome, which I represent in the title of my book *Spirituality 202* with the subtitle *Healing Cancer in Our Genes*.

The therapist who practices this philosophy always works in their therapeutic effort because they become a facilitator who directs their intention to support the interdependent rebalancing process of the universe in the sick without hindering it. Therefore, one does not mistake treating the superficial manifestations of the hologram without simultaneously correcting the roots or causes in the deeper parts of the organism. They understand that the symptoms will reappear unless the source of the unbalanced process is treated.

GUIDING THE THERAPEUTIC PROCESS WITH COMPASSION AND EMPATHY

Among the qualities that strengthen the therapist and the therapy outcome is the solidarity that the patient perceives with the compassionate intention of the therapist. This generates an inclusive bond that links the two in a triangular web that facilitates an energy exchange between the patient, therapist, and the holographic universe. This bond arises from the therapist's empathy with the patient's mistakes to create the imbalance, since the therapist can make them or has already made them.

Pity is a derogatory way to observe the patient's disease experience, in which the therapist cannot understand that it can happen to them. This vision, contrary to compassion, disrupts the energetic flow between the parts of the healing energy triangle.

Review Questions

1. How can the therapist promote well-being in the patient if they cannot eliminate the symptoms of the resulting imbalance?

2. How can we make the patient understand their responsibility at the source of their symptoms and illness without creating the inculpatory feeling of individual guilt?

3. What actions can we take to recover the understanding of our universal language? How can meditation techniques help us in this effort?

4. Can a therapist be successful if they do not practice the principles of bioethics on themselves?

5. What is the therapist's role in significantly deteriorated physical conditions, such as degenerative diseases and cancer?

6. What is the therapist's role with the patient's closest relatives?

CHAPTER 5

The Influence of the Therapeutic Environment and the Mental-Emotional State of Therapist and Patient

PREPARATION OF THE THERAPEUTIC ENVIRONMENT

Although the effect of continuity created by quantum entanglement connects all parts of the hologram, the components that interrelate in the interdimensional spaces do so by vibrational correspondence and density analogous to consonant hierarchies in music, as it occurs in the periodic table with the chemical elements. Similar vibrational states attract each other, but dissimilar ones are repelled, like oil and water. Characteristically, places, where patients with varying degrees of energy and emotional imbalance are treated, tend to accumulate vibrational mixed energy states that, for its occupants, will feel variable degrees of physical and emotional discomfort. Suppose therapists want their treatment to resonate as a melodic symphony. In that case, we must ensure that its musicians have the same training and musical experience to follow the conductor's (therapist's) direction.

For our therapeutic experience to manifest as a melodic symphony, we must eliminate the dissonant musicians and attract the most harmonic ones in their execution. The harmonious musicians are like healing consciousnesses that travel interdimensionally, helping therapists and the sick who have learned their lessons of love to regain the balance they lost in the descent into the universal journey. This disharmony appeared when they failed to direct their intention with inclusiveness. These healing consciousnesses, ascended on their three-dimensional material experience merit, have become our therapeutic guides supporting our healing intention when the patient understands their responsibility in developing the disease.

THE HARMONIZATION OF OUR THERAPEUTIC SPACES: HONORING THE INVISIBLE BEINGS WHO SHARE THEM WITH US

Although there are many traditional techniques for purification of the therapeutic space, the most effective is understanding that the entities that traditionally occupy the place have the right to share it with the therapist and patient. This is achieved with prayer and a request to ask permission to share the healing location with them.

PRAYER TO ASK PERMISSION AND SHARE ALL SPACES

I ask for permission to share this space with all the beings of the visible and invisible worlds.

And we humbly ask you to harmonize all our energies to benefit all who exist and visit this space.

Asking for permission should include the patient after explaining the therapeutic technique and before initiating contact if the therapy is manual.

The purpose of this prayer is not to displace from our healing space an inharmonious entity but to ask for consideration for the therapeutic intention and well-being of the patient. Their displacement will be voluntary if they feel out of place or uncomfortable with the vibrational state created.

Other ways of harmonizing spaces are through prayers and mantras of different religious traditions combined with aromatherapy, incense, and traditional instruments, such as Tibetan bowls and bells.

PROTECTION BY PICTORIAL IMAGES, STATUES, AND SACRED SYMBOLS

The protective effect of religious figures, whether on statues or painted images, has two benefits. First, the emotional influence on the believers of the spiritual tradition of the symbols and the vibrational impact on the environment. It is similar when we harmonize our work environment with portraits of our children, grandchildren, or pets, which have conscious and subliminal effects on our minds.

PRIVACY, VENTILATION, AND SILENCE

Typically, patients come full of apprehension associated with the expectations of therapy and the nature of their clinical condition. That is why the area should inspire security, privacy, and the absence of all sonorous junk. Depending on the patient's preference, I use relaxing, sacred, or classical music to mitigate any sound from the street or adjacent cubicles. The patient is not allowed to have their cell phone active. The temperature and ventilation of the place are pleasantly adjusted to the season's temperature. Strong air drafts are avoided. If the patient is an adult with no phobias, I prefer the patient be unaccompanied during the therapy.

PURIFICATION AND ENVIRONMENT HARMONIZATION DURING THERAPY

There must be no physical, energetic, or emotional toxins during the interview and the therapeutic act. To minimize these, I customarily place porcelain containers with sea salt or Himalayan crystals to collect negative energy fields, which I discard at the end of therapy.

PREPARATION OF THE THERAPIST

Before purifying their therapeutic place, the healer must purify their body and mind before and after each therapy. Depending on your belief, you may include personal prayers or meditations after using the prayer to ask permission to share the space with all beings.

PURIFICATION AND PROTECTION OF THE THERAPIST'S ENERGY FIELD

After the initial meditation exercise or mantras, the therapist will create an energetic sphere of protection while standing, raising their right arm with a mudra of the hand, resembling the Christian blessing, with their thumb and the next fingers stretched, and the fourth and fifth fingers bent. You are pointing toward a universal imaginary center, where the primary energy source is found. You receive from this imaginary center a pure white light and guide this light with your hand, starting on your crown and ending on it. You draw imaginary rings in spiral circles counterclockwise around your body. Finally, to clear any energy accumulated in your energy field during therapy, in the same position, collect the circles and your accumulated energy clockwise and deposit this residue in your pineal gland or send it to the center of the earth.

Between patients, you should wash your hands to purify physically and energetically. And it would be best if you never allowed the therapeutic session to be interrupted for any reason after you start.

The therapist should never offer treatments when not in optimal physical or mental condition.

THE INITIAL INTERVIEW: THE FOUNDATION OF A SUCCESSFUL THERAPEUTIC RELATIONSHIP

In my practice, the patient's interview can last two to three hours, and they always turn out differently. It is the only opportunity for the therapist to establish the patient-therapist relationship to help achieve the patient's and healer's health goals. During this experience, the roles and responsibilities of the patient and therapist are established, emphasizing that the physician is a facilitator-educator and that the patients are responsible for implementing the tools the care provider offers them. It portrays health as the patient's responsibility and not a guaranteed result of the therapist's action. It explains the difference in approaches, in which modern medicine focuses on the symptoms and disease of the patient and holistic medicine on the causes of illness that will reestablish the patient's spirit-mind-body well-being.

It explains in detail the epigenetic vision of how the quality of lifestyles can promote or deteriorate the organism's health by modifying the inappropriate information recorded in the patient's genome. They are taught to recognize the symptoms with which it presents the office as imbalances that arise as alarms to correct the cause we allowed by our negligence. It also focuses on how emotional events can be as powerful as physical events in creating symptoms and diseases.

The projection of trust and authenticity by the therapist will open all layers of information to the intuitive capability of the therapist. Intuition, although an inherent natural quality in all beings, is nurtured by the inclusive intention of the therapist and the facilitation of the patient's trust. Nonjudgmental and mindful observation of the patient will add to your intuitive effectiveness.

It encourages empathy with the patient and support in their recovery, using the therapist's and their patients' testimonies. This promotes the feeling that life is a collective experience in which we all must share solidarity that supports each other.

The patient is asked to prioritize their health goals by using the symbolism of asking for three wishes when rubbing Aladdin's lamp. The benefits of eating vegan and the advantages of saving energy expenditure and decreasing the production of toxic metabolic residues associated with ingesting animal proteins and fats are briefly discussed. Focusing the discussion respectfully according to the patient's religious beliefs will allow the patient to feel comfortable.

This interview asks about the referral source, which creates the causal relationship that led the patient to choose the therapist beyond commercial ads for miracle cures. The best relationships are established when the connection is based on the therapist's essays, books, or other patient referrals.

Review Questions

1. If we understand that the patient is not receptive or ready to facilitate the

therapeutic result, should we go ahead with therapy after the interview?

2. Why do we ask permission to use the therapy site to treat the patient?

3. In patients with diseases classified as "incurable" by modern medicine, can we give hope to the patient without guaranteeing healing?

4. What is the purpose of the patient expressing the three wishes with Aladdin's lamp? How does this help us plan therapy and clarify patient expectations?

CHAPTER 6

Refining Our Therapeutic Aim

LEARNING TO LINK THE APPROPRIATE THERAPY TO THE PATIENT NEEDS

Learning to fine-tune our therapeutic effectiveness will depend on our spiritual development and intuition and how we direct, especially the latter, based on the patient's need and not the therapist's. In my previous books, I discussed how our free will and the mistakes made in choosing the alternatives found in our interdimensional journey allowed us to recognize the most favorable decisions for the well-being of both our individual and universal holograms. The information accumulated of the most inclusive results is transmitted to the spiritual genome or akashic file, where the best options are finally saved. These wise decisions are the keys that our intuition helps to discover as light discovers the beauty hidden in the darkness of the night at dawn.

Our universal intuitive consciousness progresses in awareness as the mind discovers the upper-dimensional planes as wider concentric circles containing lower dimensions. That is why the holographic view of the upper dimensions includes the lower ones. This progression in the scope of our knowledge is what we know as spiritual wisdom that is always guided by the interdependent empathy created by love and compassion, which interlaces the universal holographic experience.

The therapeutic process is like a reunion of unconsciously created unbalanced actions that have altered the integral harmony of the hologram at some point in the journey. The rebalancing and specific affinity archived in the patient's memory (biological ADN) are reunited by the vibrational similarity of the therapist's and the patient's holograms. That is why I mentioned at the end of the previous chapter that the causal affinity that motivates the patient to choose the therapist could be decisive in the therapy outcome. This creates an energetic link between therapist and patient that facilitates the diagnostic and therapeutic certainty of the encounter. Many of our therapeutic failures result from a lack of causal affinity between the therapist and patient and not so much because of the effectiveness of therapy or the patient's receptivity.

FACTORS THAT FINE-TUNE THERAPEUTIC AIMING

THERAPIST FACTORS

1. Spiritual development
2. Intuitive maturity
3. Alimentary purity
4. Therapeutic intent

PATIENT FACTORS

1. Spiritual development
2. Causal understanding
3. Alimentary purity
4. Faith

THE SPIRITUAL DEVELOPMENT OF THE THERAPIST

The therapist awakens empathy and compassion for their patient's imbalance because they may have already gone through similar situations, which makes the therapist optimistic that they might help this patient find spiritual wellness.

It reinforces the understanding that suffering and disease are a misunderstanding of the response of the causal law of love, trying to rebalance the harmony of the universal hologram with a lesson of love that rectifies the exclusive action of the individual hologram. Therefore, the therapist does not direct their therapeutic step toward eliminating the symptom that gives the alarm of the imbalance but instead focuses on equilibrating the unevenness or cause that began the domino effect that gave rise to the disease.

INTUITIVE MATURITY

Intuitive maturity will help you choose between the therapeutic alternatives at your disposal, the most effective and the frequency you will use to facilitate the patient's well-being and the universal hologram. You will also know how far you can insist on your therapeutic action and when you should stop it and refer the patient to another therapist. As therapists, we must understand that healing can take many journeys or incarnations in the material world experience until understanding the lesson of love that the universal hologram demands for its rebalancing.

ALIMENTARY PURITY

Alimentary purity facilitates the self-healing and detoxification of the inherited mutations in your family genome and the emotional detoxification of what the patient has created in this individual holographic experience. This process will facilitate the understanding that will open interdimensional gates in the universal hologram, gradually awakening the intensity and intuitive quality that will increase its therapeutic potential to help others in their experience.

As you may remember from many spiritual traditions, "Before you know God, know yourself first." Or we can work with this one too: "Before you find your inner healer and help others, you must heal yourself first." Until this is completed, there is no diploma that any therapeutic school can issue to certify you as a healer, even if you use excellent therapeutic techniques.

THERAPEUTIC INTENTION

To better understand this part, you should

review the concept of inclusiveness versus exclusiveness in the intention and action of the individual holograms that make up our universe in chapter 2. Inclusive consciousness makes us feel "we" as a part of the virtual chain of love, and exclusiveness makes us think "me" is separated from the rest of the hologram. Inclusiveness makes us empathetic and compassionate, with imbalances that create discomfort and suffering in those who live intertwined in our universal experience. Exclusiveness makes us feel independent and isolated (insensitive) from our unbalanced effects on the universal holographic experience.

THERAPIST AND PATIENT AS FACILITATORS OF THE THERAPEUTIC OUTCOME

For the therapist, the scope of his therapeutic act should be directed by the inclusive intention, in which the main motive of the therapist is to seek the balance of the personal discomfort of their patient as an inclusive part of the universal holographic imbalance, where the priority should be the welfare of the universal hologram. As I mentioned in chapter 4, the only way to ensure this result is by creating an inclusive link in a healing triangle between the healer and patient as facilitators with the healing power of the holographic universe. Therefore, the healing energy exchange of the therapy should be directed at something other than the imbalance of the patient.

The only manner to ensure this therapeutic goal is that the therapist guides their effort without intentional interference, which I call "intentionless" intention. This openness allows the healing triangle to be guided by the spiritual hologram's universal wisdom, thus balancing the effects within the healing triangle. This final process is facilitation by the patient and therapist and healing by the universal holographic consciousness. This could explain the amplifying impact of faith and the placebo effect in modern medicine.

Review Questions

1. Review the placebo concept according to modern medicine and see how the energy-healing triangle can explain this.

2. Review Mark 10:52 (International Bible Version): "What do you want me to do for you?" he asked.

"Rabbi, I want to see," replied the blind man.

"You can go," said Jesus. "Your faith has healed you."

"At the time, he regained his sight and began to follow Jesus along the way."

3. What role does information archived in the genome have in the disease process?

4. How can we accelerate the development of our intuition in our therapeutic action?

CHAPTER 7

The Influence of Intention on Healing

INTENTION AND CAUSALITY IN HEALING: THE ROLE OF FAITH

In this chapter, I will highlight the numerous factors, such as causality and intention, that promote healing and how they interact harmoniously with the principle of faith. I will discuss the placebo effect to relate the influence of the mental process on facilitating the healing process. In a clearer perspective, I will also attempt to define the causal relationship between the disease and the healing process.

PLACEBO

Let us start with what science regards as a placebo. The origin comes from the Latin word *placére*, which means "to give pleasure." Today it is used as a name for any substance or effect, which, even without having any scientific basis, its use in patients can produce a healing effect. It is this unexplained healing result that science identifies as a placebo effect. Ironically, mainstream medicine, no matter the effectiveness of the placebo, discredits its use in clinical practice, even if superior to the drug being tested. The pharmaceutical industry has shown minimal interest in discovering the scientific reason for the placebo effect since it cannot be patented and sold.

The Science behind the Placebo Effect

These factors influence its actions:

1. *The previous therapeutic experiences of the patient*. The standard of practice in their region will influence their expectations. In occidental medicine, the more invasive and expensive the procedure is, the higher the expectation of effectiveness for the patient.

2. *The emotional and mental state of the patient*. The most mentally stable patients seem to respond better to any therapy.

3. *Spirituality is an essential part of the patient's beliefs—what I call the real power behind the throne.*

4. *The influence of the therapist-physician*. Here the placebo effect can be potentiated by references from his patients, degree of education, and specialization. Our medical system is biased because more specialization in any field guarantees a better curative effect. The white frock effect and an open and compassionate relationship between the patient and therapist that shows genuine interest in helping the patient is one of the most potent activators of the placebo effect.

Reviewing the previous factors, there is a common denominator in the healing response: the mental state or relationship between the patient and the therapist that promotes trust in the physician and confidence of the therapist in the capacity of the patient to allow the curative effect. This finally results in the physician becoming a facilitator and the patient the promoter of the recovery process of their health.

This unique relationship activates the FAITH principle:

F: Fully

A: Allowing

I: Inner Wisdom

T: to

H: Heal You

CAUSALITY IN THE DISEASE PROCESS

Wellness is the natural balance between all the parts of the universal hologram. The disease is the imbalance created by the sections of the universe looking for its equilibrium, like the symptoms our body produces to return to wellness. The sickness is the reaction of the parts of the universal hologram trying to recover its equilibrium. We can understand this as we see severe climatological changes, such as hurricanes and earthquakes, which only try to correct the imbalances created by the irresponsible actions of humanity as pathogens upon the planet. All these actions and reactions are ruled by the law of cause and effect, whose vital role is in maintaining the universe in optimal equilibrium.

The results, or effects, of the law are related to the mental intentions of conscious beings sharing the universal experience. If the purpose is guided by inclusive awareness (inclusiveness), the effects will benefit the holographic universe and are traditionally known as dharma. If the intention is steered by selfish exclusiveness, the consequences will harm the universal equilibrium, known as karma. So the awareness of our interconnectedness as a spiritual family will create a joyful experience, and the lack of this awareness (exclusiveness) results in suffering and disease.

All causes and effects are historically charted in the timeless archives of our DNA, traditionally called our Akashic records. These exist in dual formats, the spiritual and biological DNA, that interactively determine the evolutionary process of the universe.

CAUSALITY IN THE HEALING PROCESS

The healing process then becomes a process of remembering, which causes the imbalance and disease to start reversing the unbalancing process. The principal factors in initiating the healing process are accepting our responsibility for creating the original disparity and the subsequent suffering that forces us to seek its resolution.

As I describe in my books, the experiences of suffering become our guiding lessons of love that reconnect us to our inclusive awareness as a spiritual family through empathy. The FAITH principle is the facilitator that activates the memory recorded in our DNA of the rectifying healing process when the final causal process matures.

THE HEALER AS A FACILITATOR: INTENTION WITHOUT DIRECTION ("INTENTIONLESS" INTENTION)

Suppose the therapist has yet to develop their intuitive ability fully. In that case, it must be like a transparent crystal that transmits the healing energy of the universal hologram without distortion to the patient. This purity in therapeutic intent is what I call the therapeutic intention without direction (without intention [intentionless]). It links the effect of the therapeutic triangle between the universal hologram, the therapist, and the sick, ensuring a faster recovery.

THE UNCEASING (TIMELESS) EFFECT OF UNGUIDED THERAPEUTIC INTENTION

Any "intentionless" therapeutic effort has a temporal result that matures causally according to the time of the universal hologram and not the individual hologram's perception. Therefore, the facilitation of healing for the sick should be supported by the patient's patience and faith, as it will occur in God's time. That is why an "intentionless" directed therapeutic action is never wasted if we have the patience to let it bloom.

Review Questions

1. How do you explain the role of faith in a patient's recovery?

2. Why doesn't every sick person who manifests faith in the therapist get results?

3. Why does undirected intention promote healing?

4. How does the cause-and-effect law guide the patient-therapist inter-relationship?

PREPARATION DOCUMENTS

1. Prayer to Ask Permission and Share All Spaces

I ask permission to share this space with all the beings of the visible and invisible worlds.

And we humbly ask you to harmonize all our energies to benefit all who exist and visit this place.

2. Meditation: A Colorful Bath of Love

Sitting in a comfortable position, with our vertical back and head upright, let us visualize a source of strength or spiritual energy that makes us feel protected in our mirror. For example, the image of the sacred heart of Jesus or any preferred religious figure, of young, smiling appearance, with his arms open and emanating rays of multicolored light from the center of his heart toward our heart, in which there is a mirror with a little seed.

Let us understand the meaning of this exercise. The warrior represents the human manifestation of light—the force of love that reflected us from his magic mirror in his interest that we know all the immensity of his creation. Multicolored rays represent the infinite ways love can manifest or reflect among us. The seed in our hearts represents the latent form of the light warrior residing in the shadow warrior.

As these light rays fill our mirror heart, we will feel loved and protected and observe how the tiny seed begins to open, emanating multiple colors of love everywhere. Let us imagine that these colors give us a bath of loving light that reaches all parts of our body, especially those with some emotional scar, and observe how these are soothed and healed.

After this joy and well-being have filled us, we will share with the other warriors, especially those who have hurt us through ignorance of their light.

Let us visualize, then, that from our hearts, multicolored rays are reflected toward all warriors without distinction, including those who have already left our world and those who, in our perspective, have brought suffering to our lives. Let us take a few minutes in this action and then rest our minds in silence for a few extra minutes. Let us give thanks for this opportunity. Let us do this exercise every day when we get up and lie down. Finally, to keep our minds in peace, let us imagine that our thoughts are passing clouds in the sky and that our natural harmony is like the blueness of the sky. Let our ideas flow as if they were passing clouds and focus your mind on the color of the sky, the quietness of our natural mental state.

ACKNOWLEDGMENTS

Among all the travelers who have shared this endless journey in the reflecting magic mirror of my mind, I want to thank my children, their mother, my patients, and my empathetic wife, Ivette. They have so fondly supported my old man's follies.

I especially appreciate the spiritual guidance of my teachers from the Tibetan Buddhist tradition—Nyingma, the venerable Khenchen Palden Sherab Rinpoche, and Khenpo Tsewang Dongyal Rinpoche—from whom I learned the training of the mind that made it easier for me to portray the incredible wisdom of the mirror of our minds in this book.

I also recognize the significant influence on this book from the six volumes of the *One Self*, channeled by its author and channeler, Ms. Franca Rosa Canónica. I cannot fail to thank the influence of my surgical mentor and pioneer of transplant research and surgery in Puerto Rico, Dr. Eduardo Santiago Del Pin, who harvested the seed of confidence to lead me on a relentless path of seeking knowledge and truth within a humanist perspective in medicine.

Finally, my thanks to my mother, Doña Berta, for the hours she spent reading the Christian Bible during my childhood, assuring me that at some point it would support me during the challenging times of my life.

The teacher is just a disciple who likes to help others find his mastery.

Recognize that all the wisdom you have sought has always been within you.

There are no incurable diseases, only those more difficult to treat.

—Iván Figueroa Otero, MD

ENDNOTES

1. Eunsoo Won and Yong-Ku Kim, "Stress, the Autonomic Nervous System, and the Immune-kynurenine Pathway in the Etiology of Depression," *Current Neuropharmacology* 14, no. 7 (October 2016): 665–673, https://www.ncbi.nlm.nih.gov/pmc/articles/PMC5050399/.

2. Renata Roland Teixeira, et al., "Chronic Stress Induces a Hyporeactivity of the Autonomic Nervous System in Response to Acute Mental Stressor and Impairs Cognitive Performance in Business Executives," *PLoS One* 10, no. 3 (March 25, 2015), https://www.ncbi.nlm.nih.gov/pmc/articles/PMC4373764/.

3. Rasna Sabharwal, "The link between stress disorders and autonomic dysfunction in muscular dystrophy," *Frontiers in Physiology*, January, 29 2014, https://www.frontiersin.org/articles/10.3389/fphys.2014.00025/full.

4. Nicole Freeling, "How traffic jams affect heart health," UC Newsroom, December 1, 2014, https://www.universityofcalifornia.edu/news/how-traffic-jams-affect-heart-health.

ABOUT THE AUTHOR

Retired pediatric surgeon Iván Figueroa-Otero was trained in traditional Chinese medicine and acupuncture with professors from the University of Seville and became certified in medical acupuncture nationwide.

Dr. Figueroa-Otero is the author of the School of Life trilogy, with the books *Spirituality 101: For the Dropouts of the School of Life*, *Spirituality 1.2: For the Disconnected from the School of Life*, *Spirituality 103: The Forgiveness Code*, and *Spirituality 104: Reflections in My Magical Mirror*. His books have received numerous awards, such as the Benjamin Franklin

Award, NIEA Award, Readers' Favorite, Beverly Hills Award, and USA Best Book Awards, among others.